I0616339

HAPI
THE HUMAN API

HAPI
THE HUMAN API

THOMAS BURBRIDGE, M. ED

Acknowledgements

Every book is a collaboration, even one about programming people like robots. HAPI would not exist without the students who first tested the activities, laughed at the mistakes, and kept asking, "Can we do that again?" Your curiosity, energy, and willingness to debug yourselves gave this book life.

To the teachers who constantly balance creativity with classroom demands: thank you for inspiring the idea that coding can be taught without screens, expensive hardware, or frustration. You reminded me that all we need is a classroom, some space to move, and a willingness to try something new.

A special thanks to Professor HauShoe, Verlean West, Mike Ilenfeldt, and Rey Florez, who encouraged experimentation, even when it meant students marching, clapping, and pretending to be robots in the hallways. Your support made it possible to push traditional boundaries of instruction.

My colleagues in computer science and engineering education: your passion for computational thinking, design, and innovation helped shape HAPI into a tool that connects real-world programming with classroom fun.

Shae Coon – My editor. Thank you for your guidance (and patience) for this clueless writer. You have made this possible.

Finally, to my family—Brigette, Thomas, and Emma—thank you for your patience and encouragement while I turned my scattered classroom notes into a book. You kept me grounded when I disappeared into lesson planning, drafts, and doodles of footnote comics.

HAPI is for the students, but it belongs to all of us who believe in teaching with joy, humor, and the courage to try something new.

About the Author

Thomas Burbridge, M.Ed., is an educator, Navy veteran, maker, and storyteller. With more than a decade of experience teaching computer science, robotics, and engineering in the classroom, he observed that students often became frustrated when learning coding on screens too quickly.

In 2015, he created **HAPI – The Human API** as a way to strip coding down to its essentials: **step-by-step instructions, debugging, and teamwork.** By treating classmates as programmable "robots," students laugh, move, and play their way into understanding core computer science concepts.

Tom continues to write educational resources, fantasy novels, and maker guides under the banner of independent publishers. His passion for teaching is matched by his love of adventure—whether scuba diving, cycling, or tinkering in his workshop.

…end of line

Table of Contents

About HAPI

HAPI, or Human API, is a human programming language designed to introduce middle school students to the challenges of developing software on a small scale, with the ultimate goal of developing a more complex program using the instructional set outlined in this guide.

Programmer's Mindset

Getting into the Mindset of a Programmer with HAPI Programming is about breaking big problems into small, clear steps and telling the computer exactly what to do. With HAPI, you'll practice thinking like a programmer by giving precise, step-by-step instructions—just like writing a recipe that leaves no room for confusion. This mindset values logic, order, and testing ideas until they are proven effective. By learning to "program" people and objects in your environment first, you'll build the habit of planning.

Think Like A Programmer

Being a programmer is like being the boss of a super-literal robot—it will only do exactly what you tell it, no more, no less. With HAPI, you'll practice giving clear, step-by-step instructions so your "robot" (a classmate, object, or even yourself) can follow them perfectly.

This means thinking ahead, spotting problems before they happen, and fixing mistakes when they do.

The more you practice, the better you'll get at turning big ideas into small, doable steps—just like real coders do.

How to Use This Book For Teachers

Think of HAPI as a script. You'll guide students through programming each other with simple commands before they ever touch a computer.
Set roles. One student serves as the Director (writer of commands), while another

serves as the Actor (who follows the commands). Switch roles often so every student experiences both.

Model first. Demonstrate each new command with the class before assigning it.

Encourage debugging. Mistakes are expected! Have students identify what went wrong and rewrite the command sequence.

Use activities flexibly. Each section includes quick warm-ups, class activities, and longer projects. Select and choose options that fit your time and your students' readiness.

Crosswalk to standards. TEKS/Common Core connections are provided to help you tie lessons directly to learning goals.

For Students

This book is for you. You'll be learning the building blocks of computer science by treating people like programmable "robots."

Follow the roles. As an *Actor*, do exactly what the script says—even if it seems silly. As a *Director*, write your commands clearly so your Actor can succeed.

Start simple. Learn each command one at a time. Don't rush into complicated scripts until you can write the basics with accuracy.

Test and fix. If your Actor does the wrong thing, it's not their fault—it's the code! Debug by rewriting or adjusting commands.

Work together. Programming is about communication. Pay attention to how your team writes, explains, and performs instructions.

Reflect. Use the notebook pages and journal prompts to think about what worked, what didn't, and what you can try next.

Have fun. HAPI is playful on purpose. Mistakes are part of the process, and the best scripts often come from trial, error, and laughter.

Before you begin

Here are some tried and true guidelines before teaching the first lesson:

-       Write your own short HAPI program. Do this first, as there is nothing more embarrassing to a teacher than teaching something incorrectly only to have the students discover your error.

-       Run the program with another teacher or a student volunteer as the Actor.

Note any unclear commands and adjust your instructions. This "test run" helps you anticipate student questions and refine your delivery.

PART 1 - FOUNDATIONS

Getting Started

HAPI stands for Human Application Programming Interface. It's a fun way to learn how programming works without a computer.

With HAPI, people become the "computers" (called **Actors**), and other people give them exact instructions (called directors). If the **Actor** follows the instructions exactly and ends up doing what the director intended, the program works. If something goes wrong, we say the program "crashed," and we fix it just like we would in real programming.

Why Learn HAPI

Students get to see program code running in real time.

Instead of code running on a screen, watch a person act it out. It teaches the value of being exact.

Computers don't "guess" what the code intended — neither do HAPI **Actors**. It's safe to make mistakes. A mistake here means the Actor does something unexpected. Then we fix the instructions.

Using HAPI

Students begin by writing scripts based on a simple command set (page x). The scripts are written and delivered by the **Director** to the **Actor.** The Actor must listen carefully when executing the script. It is the job of the **Actor** to take the commands in a literal sense without too much interpretation.

One good example of this is when the **Director** instructs the **Actor** to 'Run Fast' after the program starts. The **Actor** executes the task and runs at his/her fastest possible speed, all while still sitting in the chair.

This adds to the comedic value of the lesson

Classroom Culture & Expectations

HAPI is not just about programming—it's about creating a classroom environment where students feel safe to take risks, make mistakes, and learn from each other. Setting clear expectations from the beginning will help students engage with confidence.

Core Expectations for Students

Precision Matters – Every command must be exact. "Walk" is not the same as "Walk three steps."

Respect the Actor – Actors can only do precisely what is coded—no extra movements, talking, or improvisation.

Safe Space – Commands must be physically secure, reasonable, and appropriate.

Active Participation – Students rotate through roles (Director, Actor, Debugger).

Celebrate Mistakes – Errors are part of debugging. Mistakes are not failures but stepping stones.

Encourage Each Other – Feedback should focus on improving the program, not criticizing the person.

Teacher Role in Culture-Building

Model Precision: When giving instructions, demonstrate clear, step-by-step directions.

Highlight Reflection: After each activity, pause and ask, *"What worked? What didn't?"*

Normalize Failure: Share your own "broken code moments." Laugh at errors and show how they lead to learning.

Promote Equity: Ensure all students have an opportunity to take on different roles. Use pair/group rotations to prevent cliques.

Establish Signals: Use agreed-upon cues for "Start," "Stop," and "Reset" to maintain order and ensure consistency.

```
Sample Classroom Norms
```

You might post these on the wall or review them often:

"Precision is kindness." **(Clear instructions prevent confusion.)**

"No extras." **(Actors only do what's coded.)**

"Debug together." **(Spot errors as a team.)**

"Mistakes move us forward." **(Celebrate errors as learning.)**

"Everyone codes, everyone acts." **(Rotate roles for fairness.)**

Common Management Challenges

Goofing Off as an Actor – Remind students that the Actor is like a "robot" following only the Director's code. Reset if needed.

Over-Explaining as Director – Encourage brevity and exact wording. Directors can revise and retry instead of adding "side notes."

Dominating Voices – Rotate leadership so all students experience different roles.

Bored Observers – Give bystanders the role of Debugger to watch for missed commands.

This section fosters a **culture of precision, patience, and playful problem-solving**—the same mindset students will need when they transition to real coding.

The Starting Position

Every HAPI program begins with the **Actor** in the **standard starting position**:

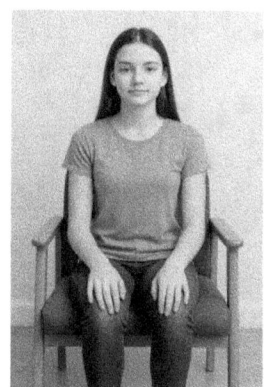

- Sitting in a chair, Arms resting on legs
- Fingers above the knees
- Eyes looking forward
- Toes pointing forward

At the end of the program, the **Actor** must return to this exact position. If they can't, the program is considered crashed.

The Flow of a HAPI Program

1. The **Director** starts by using the **Start** command.

2. **Follow Commands** – The **Actor** performs each instruction **exactly as it is written**.

3. **Return to Start** – At the end, the **Actor** returns to the starting position. This is not automatic; the **Director** must issue the commands to return to the start position..

4. **End** – The **Director** uses the End command to stop the program.

Program Example

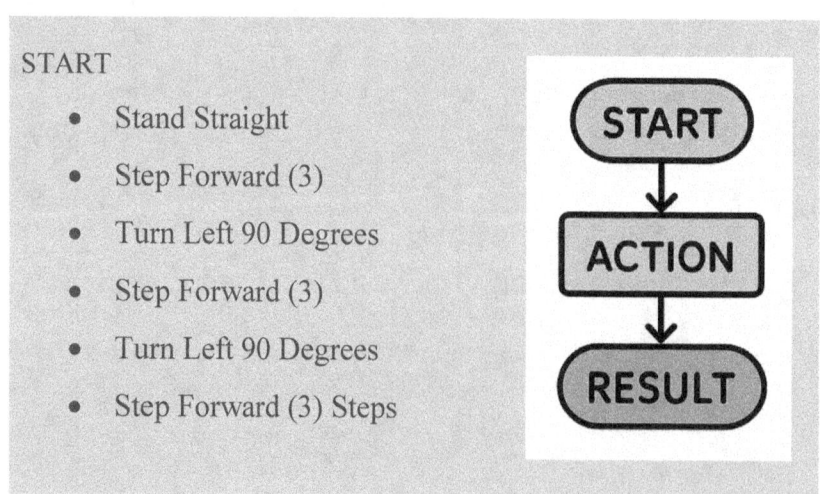

START

- Stand Straight
- Step Forward (3)
- Turn Left 90 Degrees
- Step Forward (3)
- Turn Left 90 Degrees
- Step Forward (3) Steps

- Turn Left 90 Degrees
- Step forward (3) Steps
- Turn Left 90 Degrees
- Sit Down

END

When this program runs:

1. The **Actor** starts seated in the starting position.

2. Stands up straight.

3. Steps forward (3) steps.

4. Turns left 90 degrees

5. Repeat steps 3 and 4 until the square is complete

6. Sits down.

7. End the program when the Actor returns to the starting position.

Core Concepts

Before diving into activities, students need to understand the key concepts that make HAPI effective. These concepts form the foundation of both HAPI and computer programming.

Algorithms – Step-by-Step Instructions

An **algorithm** is simply a set of clear, ordered steps to solve a problem or complete a task. In HAPI, an algorithm might look like:
1. Stand up.
2. Move Forward (3) steps.

3. Turn right 90 degrees.
4. Clap hands once.

The Actor follows these steps *exactly as written.* Missing, unclear, or out-of-order steps break the program.
Key Lesson: **Clarity and order matter.**

Actors & Directors – Roles in HAPI

Director: Writes the "code" (commands). They must be precise and detailed.
Actor: Executes the program exactly—no guessing, no extras, no shortcuts.
Debuggers (optional role): Monitor the program, identify errors, and suggest fixes.

These roles rotate, allowing all students to experience writing, performing, and troubleshooting code.
Key Lesson: **Each role mirrors a real part of computer programming.**

Commands & Syntax Basics

Commands are the "verbs" of HAPI. Each command performs a specific action (e.g., *Stand, Sit, Turn Left 90°*).

Syntax refers to the rules governing how commands are written. In HAPI:
 - Commands are written on separate lines.

-        Each command must be complete (verb + details if needed).

-        Programs start with **Start** and end with **End.**

Example Program:

```
START
   • Stand
   • Step Forward (3)
```

- Turn Right 90
- Clap Hands

END

Key Lesson: **Consistency prevents confusion.** Syntax rules make programs predictable and repeatable.

In HAPI, commands are like sentences in a story — they must follow specific rules so that the "computer" (the **Actor**) can read and understand them correctly. These rules are called programming conventions. Just like good writing has punctuation and grammar, good programming has formatting and structure. These conventions make the code easier to read and reduce the likelihood of mistakes.

Conventions

Comments (#)

Commenting on the code is like leaving notes in the margin of a difficult homework assignment. It explains what each part of the code does, so it (and others) can understand it later without having to guess. Good comments make it easier to identify and fix problems, introduce new ideas, and collaborate as a team.

A comment is a note to the director or other programmers. Actors do not read comments — they are only for humans. How to write a comment: Start the line with # and write a note after.

Example:

Actor should stand before stepping

- Stand Straight
- Step Forward (5)

Here, the **Actor** ignores the first line, but the director knows the reason for the following command.

Parentheses ( )

Parentheses are used to group actions or show priority (which action happens first).
Numbers enclosed within parentheses are repeated commands, just like in math;
what's inside the parentheses happens before what's outside.

Example:

(Turn Left 90 Degrees)

- Step Forward (5)

This tells the **Actor** to turn
before moving forward
five steps.

Spacing & Indentation

We use spaces to keep code neat and readable. Subcommands are indented under the central command to indicate their belonging.

Example:

START

- Step Forward (10)
- Turn Left 90 Degrees

END

This makes it easy to see which actions happen between **Start** and **End**.

The Starting & Ending Position

Actors begin in the standard starting position (as described in Section 1) and must return to it at the end. If they don't, the program crashes. Think of it like a video game character always starting at the "spawn point" — The **Actor** must return for the script to end.

Alternatively, the **Director** can specify a separate ending position within the code.

Pro Tip: Neat, consistent code is easier to read, easier to fix, and much less likely to cause a crash.

PART 2 - HAPI COMMANDS & SCRIPTS

HAPI Commands

In computer science, **API** stands for *Application Programming Interface.* In HAPI, the **Code API** is the "menu" of commands a Director uses to instruct an Actor. Every HAPI program relies on these commands to instruct the Actor on what to do, when to do it, and how to do it.

Structure of a HAPI Program

Every program begins with a **Start** command and finishes with an **End** command. Between Start and End, commands are listed step-by-step.

Example:

START

- Stand
- Step Forward (3)
- Turn Right 90
- Clap Hands

END

Argument Commands (Logic & Control)

These commands enable programs to make decisions or repeat actions.

If / Then / Else - *If* checks a condition. *Then* runs only if the condition is true. *Else* runs if the condition is false.
Example:

If Light = On, Then Lower Hand 2 Degrees

Else Raise Hand 2 Degrees

While

Repeats an action as long as a condition is true.

Example:

While Hand = Raised, Wave Hand

Director Commands (Main Actions)

Command	What It Does	Example
BeginSubScript	Creates reusable mini-programs	BeginSubScript Wave … End
Bend	Bends a body part	Bend Left Arm 45 Degrees
Extend	Extends a body part	Extend Arm Forward 90 Degrees
Grasp	Grabs an object	Grasp With=Right Hand CoffeeCup
Look	Moves eyes/head	Look Up 30 Degrees

Lower	Moves the body part downward	Lower Head 20 Degrees
Move	Creates a motion as indicated by the script.	Move Forward (3)
Pause	Stops all actions	Pause 00:00:05
Raise	Lifts body part	Raise Left Hand 45 Degrees
Run	Moves quickly	Run Speed(5) Steps(10)
Release	Let go of the object	Release CoffeeCup
Say	Speaks text	Say "Hello World!"
Stand	Moves into a standing position	Stand Up
Sit	Moves into sitting position	Sit Down

Step	Moves forward/back	Step Forward Steps(5)
Stop	Ends an action (not a program)	Stop Step
Touch	Touches object	Touch With Left Hand Door
Turn	Rotates body/part	Turn Right 90 Degrees

Subcommands (Details & Precision)

Subcommands refine main commands to avoid ambiguity. Without them, the Actor might guess.

Directional Subcommands

Up, Down, Left, Right, Forward, Backward

Example: Turn Left 90 Degrees

Degree (#)

Specifies exact angle.

Horizontal: DegreeH(0) = forward, DegreeH(90) = right.
Vertical: DegreeV(0) = level, DegreeV(90) = up.

Number & Counting Subcommands

Numbers following a command are repetitions of that command, rather than repeating the command line multiple times.

Number(#) → repetitions (*Clap Hands Number(3)*)
Steps(#) → movement counts (*Step Forward Steps(10)*)
Speed(#) → rate of movement (*Run Speed(5)*)

Body Part Subcommands

Arm, Leg, Foot, Head, Eyes, Hand, Finger(#), Thumb, Elbow, Knee, Ankle, Toes

```
Example: Raise Left Arm 45 Degrees
```

ObjectName: Refers to exact object names. Capitalize words.

```
Example: Grasp With=Right Hand CoffeeCup
```

Teacher Notes

Treat this section like a dictionary of commands students can reference while coding. Encourage precision: "Actors don't guess." Allow creativity but stress safety — avoid commands that strain physical limits. Reinforce structure: Start → Steps → End.

Combining Commands

What it means: Linking two or more commands together so the Actor (student or robot) does several things in a row.

Example:

- Stand Up
- Turn Right 90 Degrees
- Walk 3 Steps

Sequences

What it means: A sequence is simply the *order* in which commands are executed. Programs typically execute commands sequentially, from top to bottom.

Example:

- Sit Down
- Nod Head
- Clap Hands

If you change the order, you change the program!

Loops (repeat X times)

What it means: A loop repeats a command or a group of commands multiple times without requiring the user to rewrite them.

Example:

Repeat 3 Times:

- Clap Hands
- Nod Head

Conditionals (If/Then/Else)

What it means: Conditionals evaluate a situation and then determine the appropriate course of action.

Example:

- If light is ON, Then Turn Off. Else Turn On

Teaching tip: Have students *act these out* (like Simon Says with logic). They'll *feel* how sequences, loops, and conditionals work by being the "computer."

Scripts In Action (Unplugged)

Now that the starting position and programming conventions are known, it's time for action. In HAPI, use commands to tell the **Actor** exactly what to do. Commands are written in a specific way so the **Actor** knows:

-        What action to take

-        Which part of the body to use (if needed)

-        How to perform the action (speed, direction, distance).

The Two Golden Rules

1.   **Actors** follow commands exactly as written — no guessing. If the director says "Stand" but doesn't say "Straight," the **Actor** can stand bent over if they choose.

2.   If a command can't be done from the **Actor's** current position, the program crashes. For example, if the **Actor** cannot run while sitting down. The script must be corrected to instruct the **Actor** to first stand before continuing with the other commands.

Writing a Script

What it means: A script is a full program written step-by-step using HAPI commands. How to do it:

Begin with **START**

Add commands in sequence, loops, or conditionals.

Finish with END

Example:

```
START

    • Stand Up
    • Walk 4 Steps
    • If the chair is behind, Then Sit Down

END
```

Debugging & Testing

What it means: Debugging is the process of identifying and correcting errors in your script. Testing means running it to see if it works as intended.

Tips:

Run your script step-by-step.

Watch where it fails or does something unexpected.

Change the command(s) and try again.

Classroom Activity: Have one student be the "computer" and follow the script exactly. The rest of the group spots "bugs."

Performing in Groups

What it means: Multiple "actors" follow the same or different scripts at the same time. Why it's important: It shows how programs can run in parallel and need

coordination.
Example Group Activity:
Team A follows a script to "build a tower" (stand, pick up, place).
Team B follows a script to "test the tower" (shake, measure, clap).
Together, they simulate how large programs are built from smaller parts.

Teaching Note:

This section moves students from "single commands" into thinking like programmers — write, test, debug, and work together. It's also where teamwork and creativity shine (students can even "perform" their scripts in front of the class).

PART 3 - CLASSROOM ACTIVITIES

How Commands Work

Commands in HAPI can be detailed or straightforward:

-        **Simple Command:** Stand Straight – tells the **Actor** to stand up (straight).

-        **Detailed Command**: Turn Left 90 Degrees – tells the **Actor** exactly how far to turn.

The more specific your instructions, the more predictable the results.

Program Flow Start

1.   Use the **Start** command to begin.

2.   Commands – Write the steps in the order they should happen.

3.   Use the **End** command when the program is complete.

Note: It is permissible in HAPI to line-number the commands. This does make the code easier to track until more advanced programming skills are developed.

Example Simple Program

START

- Stand Straight
- Sit Down

END

What happens? The **Actor** stands up straight, then sits back down.

Example Detailed Program

START

- Stand Straight
- Turn Right 90 Degrees
- Step Forward (5)
- Sit Down

END

Why did this program crash?

What happens: The **Actor** stands, turns right, steps forward five steps, and sits down.

*But without a chair, the **Actor** would sit down on the ground*

Common Mistakes to Avoid

Forgetting the starting position

-       If the **Actor** isn't in the standard position before Start, the program may fail.

        Forgetting the ending position

-       If the **Actor** fails to return to the exit point properly, the program fails. Imagine if the **Director** told the **Actor** to sit without a place to sit. While this has some comedic value, it is not the desired outcome of the program.

Skipping steps. If the **Actor** is instructed to run while sitting, the program crashes. Vague instructions such as "Turn" without specifying left or right force the **Actor** to:

1.   Decides to turn in a direction (without specific instruction from the **Director**) in an infinite loop (crashes) without the ability to move on to the next instruction set.

2.   Forces the program to crash without a specific instruction set to complete that line of code.

PART 4 - STUFF FOR NERDS

Code API

API = Application Programming Interface. The Code API is the menu of commands that tell the Actor what to do, when to do it, and how to do it.

Structure of a HAPI Program

All programs begin with 'START' and end with 'END'. Commands are written step by step.

START
(commands here)
END

Argument Commands

Argument commands let programs make decisions or repeat actions.

If <condition>, Then <action>
Else <action>
While <condition>, <action>

If the chair is empty, Then Sit Down
Else Knock 3 Times
While the hand is raised, Wave Hand

Director Commands

These are the main commands used to control the Actor. Each includes description, syntax, and example.

BeginSubScript

Starts a reusable section of code.

Syntax: BeginSubScript <name>

```
Example:
BeginSubScript Wave
Raise Right Hand 90 Degrees
Lower Right Hand 90 Degrees
End
```

Bend

Bends a body part.

Syntax: Bend <Left|Right|Degree(#)>

```
Example:
Bend Left 45 Degrees
```

Extend

Extends a body part.

Syntax: Extend <Arm|Leg|Finger(#)|Degree(#)>

```
Example:
Extend Arm Forward 90 Degrees
```

Grasp

Grasps an object.

Syntax: Grasp With=<Left Hand|Right Hand>, <ObjectName>

```
Example:
Grasp With=Right Hand, CoffeeCup
```

Look

Moves eyes or head.

Syntax: Look <Up|Down|Left|Right> [Degree]

```
Example:
Look Up 30 Degrees
```

Lower

Moves a body part downward.

Syntax: Lower <BodyPart|ObjectName> [Degree]

Example:
Lower Head 20 Degrees

Pause

Pauses all actions.

Syntax: Pause HH:MM:SS

Example:
Pause 00:00:05

Raise

Moves a body part upward.

Syntax: Raise <BodyPart|ObjectName> [Degree]

Example:
Raise Left Hand 45 Degrees

Run

Moves forward quickly.

Syntax: Run [Speed(#)|Steps(#)|Distance(#)]

```
Example:
Run Speed(5) Steps(10)
```

Release

Let go of an object.

Syntax: Release <ObjectName>

```
Example:
Release CoffeeCup
```

Say

Speaks words.

Syntax: Say "text"

```
Example:
Say "Hello World!"
```

Stand

Moves into a standing position.

Syntax: Stand [Up|Straight]

Example:
Stand Up

Sit

Moves into sitting position.

Syntax: Sit [Up|Down]

Example:
Sit Down

Step

Takes a step.

Syntax: Step [Forward|Backward|Up|Down|Steps(#)|Fast|Slow]

Example:
Step Forward
Step Steps(5) Slow

Stop

Stops an action.

Syntax: Stop <Action>

Example:

Stop Step

Touch

Touches an object.

Syntax: Touch With=<BodyPart> <ObjectName>

Example:

Touch With Left Hand Door

Turn

Rotates the body or part.

Syntax: Turn <Left|Right> [Degree]

Example:

Turn Right 90 Degrees

PART 5 SCRIPTS IN ACTION

Writing a Script

Writing a script is like giving a robot exact instructions—it only knows what you tell it. When you write, focus on clarity, sequence, and detail. Start with the START command and end with END so everyone knows where the program begins and finishes. Use simple, direct commands (e.g., stand, sit, walk, raise arm) and verify that each one makes sense in order. Think of it like a recipe—if you skip steps or make them too vague, your "actor" won't know what to do.

- Tips:
- Write one command per line.
- Use indentation or spacing to keep sections neat.
- Label tricky parts with comments so that others understand your thought process.

Debugging & Testing

Debugging means finding and fixing mistakes. When actors test a script, they should follow the commands exactly as written—no guessing or improvising. If something goes wrong, that means the script needs to be fixed, not the actor. Observe:

- Did the actor get stuck? Maybe the script wasn't clear.
- Did the actor do something unexpected? That might be a missing or extra command.
- Did the actor stop too early? Perhaps the script needs a more definitive ending.

Testing should be repeated until the program runs smoothly and efficiently. Debugging is not failure—it's problem solving, and every fix makes your script stronger.

Performing in Groups

Scripts are more fun when performed together. In groups, students take turns being:

- The Director reads the script and ensures the commands are followed.

- The Actor(s) – perform the commands exactly as written.

- The Debugger(s) – observes and notes where improvements are needed.

Group performances help everyone see how scripts can be interpreted in different ways. It also encourages teamwork, since the whole group shares responsibility for making the program work. After the performance, groups can share what went well, what was confusing, and how they improved their scripts.

PART 6 - CLASS ACTIVITIES

Warm-Ups & Quick Games (5–15 minutes)

Debug the Actor

Setup: Write a short HAPI (or pseudo-code) program on the board with one or two errors.
Task: Students act it out or trace it step-by-step to find the bug.
Variation: Make it collaborative—one student reads, another "acts," others point out errors.

Missing Command Challenge

Setup: Show a program with key commands missing (e.g., "_____ Right Arm 90 Degrees").
Task: Students fill in the blanks with the correct command.
Extension: Students invent their own "missing command" puzzle for classmates.

Code Remix

Setup: Provide a basic 3–4 line program.
Task: Students change just *one* line to alter the outcome.
Goal: See how small changes create significant differences.
Structured Activities (15–30 minutes)

Actor vs. Robot Simulation

Setup: One student is the "actor," another is the "robot." Both follow a script.
Task: Compare where a human actor improvises vs. where a robot would "crash."
Reflection: Discuss why precise syntax matters.

If/Else Dance Moves

Setup: The teacher calls out conditions ("If you have red shoes, clap once. Else, spin").

Task: Students physically respond, reinforcing conditional logic.
Variation: Students write their own If/Else instructions for classmates.

While-Loop Obstacle Course

Setup: Arrange desks or cones as an "obstacle course."
Task: Students create While-loop rules, such as "While not at the wall, take two steps forward."
Reflection: Notice how loops reduce repetition in code.

Mini-Project: Command Skits

Task: Small groups write a HAPI "script" that turns into a short skit (e.g., making a sandwich, launching a rocket).

Presentation: Each group performs its "program" in front of the class.

Extension: Add debugging—audience finds where the "program" went wrong.

Collaborative Build: Classroom Machine

Setup: Teams invent a "machine" (like a Rube Goldberg chain reaction) using only written HAPI commands.
Task: Each student is a part of the machine (levers, sensors, movers).
Goal: Show how small parts working together make a system.

Multi-Day Coding Relay

Day 1: Team A starts writing a program.
Day 2: Team B continues to debug or extend.
Day 3: Team C finalizes and presents its project.

Reflection: Highlights collaboration, clarity, and the importance of comments.

Extensions for Advanced Students

Nested Loops Dance: Students design multi-layered routines with nested loops.
Program a Teacher: Students write step-by-step commands to make *you* do a silly but precise task.
Optimized Code Contest: Students take a "long" program and shorten it with loops/conditions while keeping the same output.
Inverse Debugging: Give them a final result and ask them to reverse-engineer the missing program.

Student Activities

Now it's your chance to direct, code, and test! Each challenge builds on what you've learned in earlier sections.

Director & Actor

You are the director.

1.   Place an object on the floor (any object will do).

2.   The Actor must step around the object and sit in a chair (this is NOT the starting position).

3.   The director writes the code.

4.   The Actor executes the code (bonus: get the school principal to volunteer!).

5.   Students use a regular piece of paper to write the program.

6.   Remember: All code begins with 'START' and ends with 'END'.

Ready… Set… Go!

Three-Step Program

Write a program that:
1. Starts the program.
2. Turns the Actor in place.

3. Ends the program.

Use proper comments, parentheses if needed, and indentation.

Five-Step Program

Write a program that:
1. Starts with the Actor in the starting position.
2. Has the Actor stand up and step to a specific location in the room.
3. Turns the Actor toward another direction.
4. Commands the Actor to sit back down.
5. Ends the program.

Challenge: Write it with enough detail so that any Actor could follow it exactly, even if they have never seen the room before.

Object Program

Write a program that:
1. Starts with the Actor sitting.
2. Commands the Actor to stand up.
3. Pick up an object.
4. Turn 180°.
5. Place the object somewhere else.
6. Sit back down.
7. End the program.

Extension: Write two versions of the same command:
• Without subcommands (vague)
• With subcommands (precise)

Example Prompt: Make the Actor move across the room.

Exact Turns

Direct your Actor to:
1. Stand in the starting position.
2. Turn exactly 270° to the right.
3. Turn exactly 90° to the left.
4. Sit down.

Don't act it out yourself — write it as a HAPI program and give it to someone else to follow.

Debugging Challenge

Run a short program with a partner as the Actor.

If something goes wrong:
• Watch closely and take notes.
• Fix it using at least two tips from this section.
• Run it again.

Apply the Terms

1.   Pick any five terms from this section.

2.   Write a short HAPI program that demonstrates each one.

3.   Work with a partner to test and check for understanding.

PART 7 - NERD TERMS DEFINED

These definitions are written for beginners, but teachers can expand on them with examples.

Actor - The person is following the HAPI program's commands.

Tip: The actor acts like a computer — no guessing, no extra steps.

Director - The person who writes and gives the HAPI program to the actor.

Tip: The director's job is to be exact.

Script - The written list of HAPI commands that the **Actor** follows.

Tip: Always start with 'Start' and finish with 'End'.

Abstraction - A simpler way to represent something more complex.

```
Example: Saying "Step to the table" instead of listing
every single step and foot placement.
```

Accessibility - Designing instructions or environments that are accessible to all people, including those with disabilities.

```
Example: Writing clear commands without assuming the
Actor can see a specific landmark.
```

Algorithm - A list of steps to complete a task. Example: A recipe is an algorithm for cooking.

Block-Based Programming Language - A programming language that allows users to program by moving and connecting blocks instead of typing text.

Examples: Scratch, Blockly. Note: HAPI uses text commands, but block-based languages use the same logical thinking.

Bug - An error in the program that causes it to behave differently than expected.

Example: Forgetting to tell the **Actor** to stand before running.

Call (a Variable) - Using a stored piece of information in the program.

Call (a Function) - Telling the program to run a section of code (a function) when needed.

Command - A single instruction in the program. Example: Stand Straight

Data - Information used in the program. Example: The number of steps to take.

Debugging - Identifying and resolving issues within the program.

Define (a Function) - Create a new action that can be reused later in the program.

Event - Something that happens and triggers an action in the program.

For Loop - A command that repeats steps a set number of times.

Function - A reusable block of code that performs a specific task

If-Statement - A command that makes a decision: If this is true, then do that.

Iteration - Doing something over and over in a loop.

Loop - A set of actions repeated until told to stop.

Parameter - Extra information gives a command to customize it.

Example: Turn Left 90 Degrees — the 90 Degrees is the parameter.

Program - The complete list of instructions for the **Actor**

Variable - A placeholder for information that might change.

While Loop - A loop that repeats as long as a specific condition is true.

PART 8 - GUIDE TO TEACHING HAPI

This section is for teachers and facilitators who will be introducing HAPI to students. It provides pacing suggestions, classroom management tips, and strategies for adapting lessons to meet the diverse needs of students.

Purpose of HAPI in the Classroom: HAPI helps students understand the logic and structure of programming before using a computer. Practice writing clear, step-by-step instructions. Develop problem-solving, teamwork, and debugging skills in a low-pressure, hands-on way.

Recommended Grade Levels: Best for grades 5–8. Can be adapted for younger students by simplifying commands or for older students by adding complexity and decision-making (If/Else statements, loops).

Materials Needed: An open floor space or a clear classroom area. Chairs for the starting position. Everyday classroom items (pencils, cups, books) for object interaction. Whiteboard or projector to display example scripts. Printed HAPI command list and subcommand reference sheet.

Suggested Lesson Flow: Each lesson should include three parts:

Warm-Up (5 min) – Review one HAPI concept or command.

Instruction & Modeling (10–15 min) – Teacher demonstrates writing and running a short program with a student **Actor.**

Student Practice (20–25 min) – Students work in pairs or small groups, switching roles between director and **Actor.**

Debrief (5 min) – Discuss challenges, successes, and strategies used.

Classroom Management Tips

A challenge for all teachers.

1.   Set clear physical boundaries. Mark a "stage" area for **Actors** to perform.

2.   Rotate roles often. Every student should be both the Director and the **Actor** multiple times.

3.   Encourage precise language. Remind students, "No guessing, no adding extra steps."

4.   Celebrate mistakes. Treat errors as learning opportunities for debugging.

Differentiation Strategies for Struggling Students:

Provide partial scripts for them to complete. Limit commands to 3–4 simple steps.

For advanced students: Introduce multiple **Actors** working in sync. Use If/Else and While loops to add complexity. Require **Actors** to interact with multiple objects.

For English Language Learners: Provide visuals for commands. Pair with a supportive peer. Use physical demonstrations before running scripts.

Formative Assessment Ideas: Observe students as they direct and act, noting the clarity and accuracy of their commands.

Summative: Have students write a complete HAPI program and run it successfully without correction.

Self-Assessment: Students reflect on which commands were effective and where adjustments are needed.

Sample Multi-Day Pacing

Day 1: Introduction, Starting Position, and basic movement commands (Stand, Sit, Step).

Day 2: Adding precision with subcommands (degrees, steps, directions).

Day 3: Control flow commands (If, Then, Else, While).

Day 4: Debugging and troubleshooting practice.

Day 5: Student-created programs and showcase.

5 Minute Warm-ups

Warm-Up 1 – Fix the Script: Display a short HAPI script with a mistake.

Example:

```
START
    • Step Forward 5 Steps
    • Sit Down
END
```

Problem: The **Actor** never stood up before stepping, and the **Actor** did not return to the chair; instead, they sat on the floor (crash).

Students rewrite the script to make it work.

Warm-Up 2 – One Command Only: Give students one command (e.g., "Turn Right 90 Degrees") and have them act it out together.

Warm-Up 3 – Fill in the Blank Show part of a program with missing commands.

Example:

```
START
    • Stand Straight _____
    • Sit Down
END
```

Students fill in a reasonable command for the blank.

Warm-Up 4 – Subcommand Match Write commands on one set of cards and subcommands on another. Students match them correctly.

```
Example: Step → Steps(3).
```

Warm-Up 5 – Human Compiler: The **Director** reads a script aloud slowly, and students (as **Actors**) carry out the commands as a group without talking.

Exit Tickets (5 Minutes)

Exit Ticket 1 – Translate It Write a real-world instruction in plain English (e.g., "Get the book from the desk") and have students rewrite it as a HAPI program.

Exit Ticket 2 – Debug It: Give students a script that doesn't work. They circle the line causing the crash and explain why.

Exit Ticket 3 – Explain the Command: Pick a command from today's lesson and have students write a one-sentence explanation of what it does.

Exit Ticket 4 – Write & Swap Students write a 3-step HAPI program, swap with a partner, and see if it works.

Exit Ticket 5 – Self-Check Students' answer: One thing they learned today. One command they feel confident using. One thing they want to practice more.

Quick Activity

Pick one warm-up and one exit ticket from this section to use tomorrow. Keep them simple — the goal is quick engagement and fast feedback.

PART 9 - EASY SUBPLANS

This section is designed so any substitute teacher can step in, pick up the guide, and run a productive HAPI class — even if they've never used HAPI before.

Key Notes for the Substitute

HAPI is a classroom "acting game" that teaches programming logic without the use of computers. Students take turns as directors (giving commands) and **Actors** (following commands exactly).

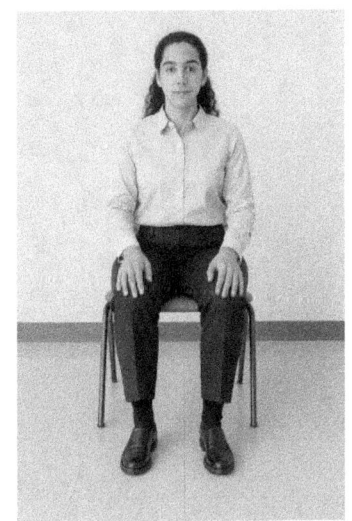

Programs begin with **a Start** statement and finish with **an End** statement.

The **Actor** begins in a starting position, sitting upright in a standard chair, facing forward, with Arms on Legs, Fingers above the knees, and Toes forward.

Materials Provided in the Companion Kit

Additionally, a printed HAPI Command List (basic commands and subcommands).

Sample short scripts for demonstration.

A few small classroom objects (pencils, cups, books) for interaction commands.

A roll of tape or cones to mark an acting space.

For 55 minutes, use 45-minute pacing with the following:

Instruct the class on the basics of HAPI. Stress the rules by providing an example. When the director instructs the **Actor** to stand without specifying "up" or "straight," the **Actor** stands but remains bent over, as if sitting with their legs straight.

Hand out the student list of commands (included with the book).

51

Select two students (those who are paying attention).

Give them one of the 'It's your turn' options and have them act it out (5 minutes).

Once complete, ask for four additional people to play while the class watches.

Then, everyone develops a basic script and performs it.

PART 10 - RUBRICS

Use this rubric to assess student-created HAPI programs. Total: 10 points.

Category	2 pts	1 pt	0 pts
Clarity	Commands are precise and easy to follow	Some commands unclear	Commands are confusing or missing
Accuracy	Script follows syntax and structure	Minor syntax errors	Major errors; doesn't run
Creativity	Original, fun, or challenging script	Some creativity	Fundamental, no effort
Readability	Script is adequately spaced and reads easily	Some spacing for reading	Hard to read and follow
Teamwork	The group collaborated effectively	Some imbalance	One person did all the work

Performance can be assessed during live activities and added to the rubric as needed.

PART 11 - TEACHER TOOLS

Lesson Plans & Pacing Guides

Daily / Weekly Breakdown (Sample: Week 1–3 Progression)

Week 1: Getting Started

Day 1 (Intro): Introduce *Actors* and *Directors.* Model the START → END structure.
Day 2: Teach **Stand / Sit / Walk** commands. Have students pair up and write 3-step programs.
Day 3 (Guided Practice): Debug Theater—students intentionally write a broken script for peers to fix.
Day 4–5 (Project): Challenge groups to create a short skit (6–8 steps). End with class performance.

Week 2: Turning & Raising Arms

Day 1–2: Introduce **Turn Left/Right Degrees** and **Raise Arm Degrees.** Demonstrate 90° vs. 45°.
Day 3: Warm-up game: "Compass Turns." The teacher calls out degrees, and the Actors rotate accordingly.
Day 4: Students write a program where an Actor navigates an obstacle course.
Day 5 (Project): Showcase "Robot Dance Moves."

Week 3: Conditionals (If/Then/Else)

Day 1 (Intro): Teach If/Then/Else with a light switch demo.

Day 2: Practice: If the Actor sees a red object, walk three steps; else sit down.

Day 3: Debugging challenge—scripts with missing or incorrect conditions.

Day 4–5 (Project): Small groups create "Choose Your Own Adventure" skits using conditions.

Substitute-Friendly Versions

Each substitute plan includes:

Clear objectives (e.g., "Students will create a 5-step program using Stand, Sit, and Turn.")
Minimal prep (blank paper, projector optional).
Scripted teacher instructions (so a sub with no coding knowledge can succeed).
Built-in assessment (students turn in scripts or reflections at the end).

Example Sub Plan

Warm-Up: "Write a 3-step morning routine (no wrong answers)."

Activity: In pairs, one student plays the role of the Actor, and the other plays the role of the Director. Write a 5-step HAPI script. Swap roles.
Exit Ticket: "What was one mistake your Actor made? How did you fix it?"

Reflection Journal Prompts (Examples)

- What was the funniest error you made today, and how did you fix it?

- How does being a Director feel different from being an Actor?

- If computers followed your script today, what would have gone wrong?

Exit Ticket Examples

Define: What does "Debugging" mean?

True/False: (T)

Every HAPI program must begin with a **START** and finish with an **END** command.
Quick Script: Write three commands that would make your Actor clap their hands.

HAPI Standards Alignment with Activity Mapping

Author's Note – It was not an afterthought that this part is here. Back when I originally wrote this document (2015), I had to do daily lesson plans, including TEKS (in Texas). It was a P.I.T.A. and REALLY soured me on certain types of (micro) managers. So to satisfy the powers that be, I included TEKS and CCSS standards.

This document lists all TEKS numbers and Common Core State Standards (CCSS) aligned with HAPI (Human API) activities, with specific HAPI sections and activities mapped to each standard for lesson planning.

Technology Applications TEKS

§126.14 (c)(1) Creativity and Innovation: Section 5 – Degree Compass & Visual Reference (creative programs)
Activity – Dance Compiler (modularity & choreography)

§126.14 (c)(2) Communication and Collaboration: Section 3 – Programming Each Other (unplugged teamwork)
Activity – Debug Theater (peer communication while fixing scripts)

§126.14 (c)(3) Research and Information Fluency: Section 6 – Debugging Code (plan, test, refine scripts)
Activity – Missing Code Challenges (iterative problem-solving)

§126.14 (c)(4) Critical Thinking, Problem Solving, and Decision Making: Section 4 – Translating Code (If/Then, While loops)
Activity – Human Maze Navigation (decision-based movement)

§126.14 (c)(5) Digital Citizenship: Section 2 – Programming Conventions & Commands (precision and clarity)

§126.14 (c)(6) Technology Operations and Concepts: Section 4 – Translating Code (structured syntax practice)
Activity – Human Sorting Algorithm (algorithm execution)

59

CTE: Principles of Applied Engineering / Robotics TEKS

§127.447 (c)(2) Communication: Writing structured HAPI scripts (technical communication)
Activity – HAPI Orchestra (coordinated instructions)

§127.447 (c)(3) Problem Solving: Section 6 – Debugging Code (error analysis & correction)
Activity – Debug Theater (broken scripts to fix)

§127.447 (c)(4) Safety, Health, and Environment: All unplugged activities require safe movement awareness
Set up protocols in Maze and Dance activities.

§127.447 (c)(5) Engineering Design: Section 7 – It's Your Turn (design & test original scripts)
Activity – Robot Factory (subroutines & design process)

§127.447 (c)(6) Emerging Technologies: Activity – Emoji Interpreter (symbolic abstraction)

§127.447 (c)(7) Critical Thinking: Activities – If/Else Simon Says, Floss Dance Challenge

§127.447 (c)(8) Teamwork and Leadership: Director/Actor roles in every section
Activity – Parallel Maze Race (leadership & synchronization)

Mathematics TEKS

§111.27 (b)(1) Mathematical process standards: Section 5 – Degree Compass (precision & measurement)

§111.27 (b)(2)(B) Represent problems with equations/inequalities: Activity – Human Calculator (variables & expressions)

§111.27 (b)(3)(C) Use variables in problem-solving: Activity – Treasure Hunt (conditional variables)

§111.27 (b)(4) Proportionality, ratios, rates: Looped steps and turns in dance activities

Science TEKS

§112.18 (b)(2)(A) Plan and implement investigative procedures: Debugging sessions treated as experiments

§112.18 (b)(3)(B) Use models to represent systems: Actors represent algorithmic systems in Sorting or Pong

§112.18 (b)(4)(A) Collect and analyze information: Journals in Section 6 – reflection on debugging results

English Language Arts TEKS

§110.22 (b)(6) Writing expository texts: Students explain their code logic in journals

§110.22 (b)(7) Oral and written communication of ideas: Pair programming & presentation of HAPI scripts

§110.22 (b)(9) Use of precise language for task execution: Section 2 – Commands must be unambiguous

Physical Education TEKS

§116.23 (b)(1)(A) Demonstrate competency in movement patterns: All physical HAPI activities (Simon Says, Maze, Dance)

§116.23 (b)(2)(C) Apply movement concepts and principles: Dance Compiler & Floss Dance Challenge

Common Core Mathematics

CCSS.MATH.PRACTICE.MP1: Maze Navigation (persevere in solving)

CCSS.MATH.PRACTICE.MP4: Human Pong (modeling a system)

CCSS.MATH.PRACTICE.MP5: Using tape, props, and music as strategic tools

CCSS.MATH.PRACTICE.MP6: Precise steps & degrees in scripts

CCSS.MATH.PRACTICE.MP7: Sorting Algorithm (use of structure)

Common Core ELA

CCSS.ELA-LITERACY.W.6.2: Write explanations of debugging processes

CCSS.ELA-LITERACY.SL.6.1: Collaborative unplugged programming sessions

CCSS.ELA-LITERACY.L.6.6: Acquiring coding-specific vocabulary (loop, variable, debug)

CSTA Computer Science Standards

1B-AP-08: Comparing algorithms in Sorting vs. Maze activities

2-AP-10: Flowcharts for HAPI scripts in Section 4

2-AP-12: Floss Dance Challenge (loops + conditionals combined)

Glossary of Commands & Terms

Actor – The student who performs commands exactly as written, without adding personal interpretation or embellishment.

API (Application Programming Interface) – A set of instructions or "menu of commands" that tells someone (or something) exactly what to do. HAPI is a *human version* of this.

Bug – A mistake in the program that causes the Actor to do something unintended.

Command – A single instruction written in HAPI language (e.g., "Turn Right 90 Degrees").

Conditional (If/Then/Else) – A statement that lets the program make decisions depending on conditions.

Debugging – The process of finding and fixing mistakes in a script.

Director – The student who writes the commands and controls the Actor.

End – A required command that closes every HAPI program.

Loop – A command structure that repeats a set of instructions multiple times.

Script – A sequence of HAPI commands written from START to END.

Start – A required command that begins every HAPI program.

Syntax – The exact spelling, structure, and order of a command so it can be understood.

Variable (advanced) – A placeholder for a value that can change, such as "steps = 3." (Introduced in extensions.)

References / Further Reading

HAPI QuickStart Guide – Jumpstart the activities with a few basic instructions.
    Available September 2025.

Unplugged Computer Science

CS Unplugged (csunplugged.org) – Free activities that teach computing without a computer.
Wing, J. M. (2006). *Computational Thinking.* Communications of the ACM.

Coding Basics

Python.org (Beginner's Guide) – Connecting HAPI commands to real-world programming.
Scratch (scratch.mit.edu) – Visual block coding for beginners.

Education & Pedagogy

Papert, S. (1980). *Mindstorms: Children, Computers, and Powerful Ideas.* MIT Press.
Resnick, M. (2017). *Lifelong Kindergarten: Cultivating Creativity Through Projects, Passion, Peers, and Play.* MIT Press.

Robotics & Making

LEGO Education Activities – Bridging unplugged coding with robotics.
Arduino.cc – Transitioning from unplugged HAPI logic to microcontroller coding.